CAGE

Oxford Studies of Composers (18)

CAGE

PAUL GRIFFITHS

London

OXFORD UNIVERSITY PRESS

NEW YORK   MELBOURNE

1981

Oxford University Press, Walton Street, Oxford OX2 6DP

LONDON GLASGOW NEW YORK TORONTO

DELHI BOMBAY CALCUTTA MADRAS KARACHI

KUALA LUMPUR SINGAPORE HONG KONG TOKYO

NAIROBI DAR ES SALAAM CAPE TOWN

MELBOURNE AUCKLAND

and associate companies in

BEIRUT BERLIN IBADAN MEXICO CITY

ISBN 0 19 315450 1

© Paul Griffiths 1981

British Library Cataloguing in Publication Data

Griffiths, Paul
    Cage. – (Oxford studies of composers; 18)
    1. Cage, John
    I. Series
    780'.92'4   ML410.C24   80-41662
    ISBN 0-19-315450-1

*Printed in Great Britain
at the University Press, Oxford
by Eric Buckley
Printer to the University*

PREFACE

IN an earlier study in this series, on Boulez, I mentioned the necessarily tentative nature of any work on a living composer. Cage has enjoyed a longer and considerably more abundant creative career than Boulez, but even so it would be unwise to regard the present assessment as final. Though now of an age when any other composer would have settled into a 'late period', he retains the unfettered inquisitiveness of youth and may yet surprise us with another turn of direction, as so often in the past.

My thanks are due to him for checking and correcting my list of his works, and also to Peters Edition Ltd (London) for the loan of scores. Music examples are notated at sounding pitch and are reproduced by kind permission of the publishers, Henmar Press Inc., New York.

for Rachel

a Valentine in Season

CONTENTS

CHROMATIC STUDIES

CAGE'S reputation is that of the apostle of indeterminacy in music, and perhaps also of irreverence. He was the composer who, in 1951, first allowed creative decisions to be made according to the dictates of chance. He was the man who, in his *4′ 33″* of 1952, interposed nothing between his audience and silence. And he is the idealist who for thirty years has been teaching, in lectures and by example, the Zen virtues of a purposeless art. The influence of his ideas during this period cannot be questioned, and yet the relative neglect of his earlier music has often led to a misrepresentation of his attitudes. Undoubtedly he would not have taken his chosen path if he had not contained within himself the iconoclast and the humorist, but it is not enough to categorize his activities as all skits and japes. The genial sceptic is also the serious searcher with his own aims, and only in the light of those aims is it possible to understand how the same man could be the author of more than sixty fully determined compositions in addition to a large output of music dependent in some manner on chance. The revolution of 1951 was no volte-face but rather a further step, radical indeed, towards the goal of artistic self-renunciation which Cage appears to have been pursuing from the first. His earlier works reveal a fascination with strict compositional systems which would make the process of creation virtually automatic, and hence independent of personal taste. Such an objective mode of composing required also the absence of a distinctive style, and Cage seems always to have been at some pains to avoid forming his own manner. Whenever one of his systems became sufficiently well established and sufficiently rich to provide the basis of a style, he dropped it for another.

The first compositional method that Cage introduced was a simple non-serial control of chromatic polyphony, employed in three works of 1933–4: the Sonata for Two Voices, the Composition for Three Voices, and the Solo with Obbligato Accompaniment (also three-part). Each line in these works is confined to a chromatic range of two octaves, and therefore to twenty-five different pitches. Cage applies the principle that repetitions are to be avoided, both within and between voices, as shown in the first section of the Composition:

Ex. I

Here, as in the several sections that follow continuously, each part runs through its repertory of twenty-five pitches (with very minor deviations: the third voice in Ex. I borrows one note, its final G♭, from the next section). There are thirteen pitches held in common by the three parts (d–d′), and so each of these occurs three times in the section; but close repetitions are avoided by distributing the occurrences evenly among the three bars (there is, of course, a fourth G♭, placed in the first bar). As if this austere handling of pitch were not enough, the absence of instrumentation, dynamic markings, and phrasing indications adds to the flat impression of a speculative construction, an impression further enhanced by the choice of accidentals. All these features are found also in the Sonata for Two Voices and in the Solo with Obbligato Accompaniment, together with those rhythmic constraints which add yet another level of objectivity. In the case of the Composition, the three fragments marked I, II, and III (they are so marked in the score) return in each succeeding section with transpositions and minor changes of note value, while the Solo with Obbligato Accompaniment sports a variety of rhythmic canons.

These severe and mechanical polyphonies had been immediately preceded by a somewhat more capricious work, the Sonata for solo clarinet (1933), which contains the seeds of the constructions that followed. The last of its three short movements is contained within the same twenty-five-note range used in the top part of the Composition for Three Voices, but the non-repetition rule is not enforced, and, although the first movement is an exact pitch-class retrograde of the last, it ranges well beyond the two-octave limit there imposed. The middle movement, surprisingly at this early date, is a miniature essay in twelve-note serialism, with a prime form followed by an inversion, a retrograde, a slightly altered retrograde, a barely related twelve-note set, and a retrograde inversion. And this centrepiece is placed in relief not only by the pitch-class correspondences between the fast outer movements but also by their notated formal divisions. Both are separated by double barlines into five sections, a structure embodied in the first by an ABABA arrangement of rhythms (the second B is approximately the retrograde of the first, and the two later A segments are varied condensations of the first). But, in a manner to be found in many of Cage's later works, the finale ignores the notated rhythmic structure, proceeding largely in even quavers. Ex. 2 shows for comparison two pitch-class equivalent sections, the second segment from the first movement (Ex. 2a) and the fourth from the finale (Ex. 2b):

Ex. 2
(a)

(b)

All the compositions so far discussed date from the period when Cage, then in his early twenties, was having lessons with Henry Cowell, who, as a fellow Californian and fellow musical radical, must have felt some sympathy with Cage's wish to invent his own language from first principles. There was bound to be less encouragement from Schoenberg, with whom Cage studied from 1935 to 1937. As Cage has often recalled, Schoenberg declared that his pupil's lack of feeeling for harmony was bound to create difficulties, and so the young composer resolved to give his attention instead to matters of rhythm. The twenty-five-note system was dropped, and the slow movement of the

Clarinet Sonata was not followed by any more such nearly classical, if very modest, uses of serialism. Rather, Cage began to use the series as a source of smaller units in such works as the Two Pieces for piano of *c*.1935. In having no markings for phrasing or dynamics, and no sharps, these resemble the works of 1933–4, but in construction they are quite different. Both pieces are built entirely from a small repertory of motifs which remain intervallically and rhythmically fixed; they are all present at the opening of the first piece:

Ex. 3

In this earliest published piano work Cage uses the instrument consistently in two-part counterpoint, with passages of hocketing in the faster second piece, where the triplets are excluded and running quavers dominate the texture. The material is extraordinarily limited, and its organization scarcely gives a feeling of freedom: not long after Ex. 3, for instance, the left hand repeats the same rising fifth twelve times, and this is only an extreme point in a chromatic ostinato fabric which has absolutely nothing in common with other serial music being composed in the 1930s.

The ostinato technique is even more single-mindedly applied in those contemporary pieces in which Cage dispenses entirely with harmony by confining himself to percussion. In the Quartet (1935) and the Trio (1936) concentration on rhythm is complete: the Quartet does not even stipulate what instruments are to be used, and the Trio eschews all the sonic flamboyance of Varèse's recent *Ionisation* (1929–31) in keeping to meagre resources of skin and wood. The waltz finale from the Trio, later incorporated in *Amores* (1943), is typically curtailed in sound and structure. Ex. 4 shows the opening of the movement, exposing the two patterns on which it is based, and Ex. 5 is a diagrammatic representation of the whole waltz, with rests indicating the time intervals by which rhythmic units are delayed after the first beat of the bar:

Ex. 4

Ex. 5

There are eighteen appearances of *a*: three on the first beat, three after one quaver, three after one crotchet, and so on. These are so arranged as to make a development from simple to complex in two stages, the first beginning with six bars of unsyncopated *a*, the second with six bars of *a* on the second quaver of the bar (bars 14–19). The *b* figures are more common in the second phase, where they imitate the triple form of the *a* patterns (bars 20–3; note also bars 24–8).

In its obsessive patterning, its hypnotic tranquillity, and its neglect of pitch, Cage's percussion music of 1935–6 is perhaps further removed from western norms than anything composed up to that date. There would have been stimulus from the study of non-European music that he undertook under Cowell, but such a piece as the 1936 waltz is no more Asian or African than it is European. Cage merely erects a simple structure from the most rudimentary rhythmic units and leaves it at that. Thirty years later Steve Reich and others were to create much more complicated music on the basis of similar ostinatos, but Cage had no wish to develop his basic ideas. Instead he changed tack again, and in 1938 returned to pitched material in the manner of the earlier piano pieces to create three unusually ambitious works: the Five Cummings Songs, *Metamorphosis* for piano, and the Music for Wind Instruments.

Cage signalled his new pretensions by giving *Metamorphosis* the designation Op. 2, which appears with hindsight as a declaration of intent quite unusually out of character. The opus consists of five pieces, all based on serial fragments containing from two to five

5

pitches. These fragments are endlessly transposed and subjected to internal octave changes, but they retain the same rhythmic shapes throughout the volume, so that, for instance, the fourth piece is a race of major seconds in falling quavers while the fifth (Ex. 6) combines these units with an equally fixed, though sometimes harmonized, three-note pattern:

Ex. 6

Similarly disconcerting in their calculated simplicity and disregard for serial orthodoxy are the songs and the wind pieces, the former even including one number ('In just Spring') which is a near monotone chant for the voice. Like *Metamorphosis*, these two other sets of 1938 are constructed from unchanging serial elements in a manner that obviously relates directly not only to the technique used in 1935 (in the Three Pieces for flute duet as well as in the piano pieces) but also to the procedure with rhythmic motifs in the percussion works. But once again Cage was to abandon a style as soon as he had established it.

RHYTHMIC SYSTEMS

IN 1937, soon after the composition of his first percussion works, Cage wrote a lecture, 'The Future of Music: Credo', which is a Varèse-like prophecy concerning the great benefits to come from the use of 'electrical instruments which will make available for musical purposes any and all sounds that can be heard'. In the light of his subsequent work it is interesting to note how much attention he gives in this lecture to the structuring of the new materials, deciding that: 'New methods will be discovered, bearing a definite relation to Schoenberg's twelve-tone system and present methods of writing percussion music and any other methods which are free from the concept of a fundamental tone.' It is also noteworthy that at this early date he remarks upon an analogy between musical and social systems: 'Schoenberg's method is analogous to modern society, in which the emphasis is on the group and the integration of the individual in the group.' This line of thinking would later gain a position of great importance in his creative aims, but for the moment he was more concerned with enlarging the means open to music and with finding appropriate methods of structuring those means.

He did this first in *Imaginary Landscape No. 1* (1939), which was the first notated piece by anyone for electrical apparatus other than specially manufactured instruments such as the ondes martenot: it calls for two players with frequency records and turntables, as well as a cymballist and a pianist. Though sometimes claimed as the earliest example of live electronic music, *Imaginary Landscape No. 1* was originally intended for broadcast performance and Cage has preferred to give the electronic component the modest denomination of 'sound effects'. And indeed this is quite a modest piece. The frequency records can give only constant tones or siren-like glissandos, obtained by changing the turntable speed while a record is being played, and the piano part is restricted to three 'muted' notes, performed with the palm on the strings, and a sweep of the bass strings with a gong beater (following Cowell's example, Cage uses the term 'string piano' for a part requiring the player to operate inside the instrument). Thus the material of *Imaginary Landscape No. 1* is very limited, enough to make the bright prophecies of 1937 sound rather hollow, though Cage does create here a novel kind of form which, with some adaptation, would suit him for the next dozen years. The bare events of the piece are fitted into a pre-arranged time scheme in which there are four sections of three times five bars, these separated by interludes growing progressively from one bar to three and concluded with a four-bar coda. Ex. 7 shows the beginning, the crosses in the second gramophone part indicating gradual changes of speed from 33 to 78 rpm:

Ex. 7

The second section is a variation of the first, the third introduces new ideas, and the last is a sort of recapitulation.

In his next work, *First Construction (in Metal)* for percussion sextet (also 1939), Cage extends the rhythmic-structure technique of *Imaginary Landscape No. 1* and creates a very much richer musical development. The whole work is based on the durational proportions 4:3:2:3:4, for not only are the sixteen large sections grouped according to this plan but also each section consists of sixteen bars similarly grouped, so that there is an immediate correspondence of structure between the small units and the whole form. The first sixteen-bar section shows the proportional divisions very clearly:

Four such sections make up the exposition of the work, and each of them is developed in turn in the four 'super-sections' of the development, these corresponding to the proportions 3 : 2 : 3 : 4; there is finally a nine-bar coda.

In developing his material Cage is as schematic as in constructing the form. Each of the four phases of the development keeps broadly to the rhythmic ideas and the sounds of the corresponding exposition section. Thus, for example, the development of Ex. 8, occupying sections 5–7, begins with the oxen bells repeating the string piano's very first motif, and the exposition's growth in diversity of rhythm and sound is renewed on a larger scale in the development: sections 1 and 5–7 are based largely on the four motifs announced by the string piano in the first three-and-a-half bars, and each subsequent section introduces a further four motifs which are taken up in the associated phase of the development, so that both exposition and development gradually build up a repertory of sixteen motifs. The organization of sonority is similar. Cage has said that he began with the idea that each player should have sixteen sounds, introducing four new ones in each section of the exposition (and, though this is not stated, doing the same in each super-section of the development). He confesses that this plan was not carried through rigorously, though the minor imperfections barely alter the effect of a spreading in pitch and timbre as well as in rhythmic complexity. In Ex. 8, for instance, five of the six players keep to their repertories of four sounds each (the exception is the third, and the thundersheets are discounted from the reckoning), and these repertories, with the oxen bells now increased to the proper four, are adhered to throughout sections 5–7.

In using a modest array of basic elements the *First Construction* does not depart from earlier works by Cage, but its thorough-going rhythmic structure and its complex elaboration were new, their origins to be found in other American music and further afield. The idea of using blocks of time, introduced in *Imaginary Landscape No. 1*, may well have come from the work of Antheil, and through him from such Stravinsky scores as *Les Noces* and *The Rite of Spring*. Antheil's *Ballet mécanique* (1924), scored at different times for various assortments of pianos, pianolas, and percussion, would seem to be a very direct ancestor of Cage's *First Construction*, not only in its instrumentation and its abundant ostinatos, but also in its dependence on what Antheil called the 'time-space' principle, by which musical structure is geared to lengths of time as a building to its girders. Cage would almost certainly have been aware of Antheil's work, and he must have known something too of Balinese music, about which Colin McPhee had written an article in the influential journal *Modern Music* in 1935: the coexistence of separate temporal levels in the *First Construction*, as at the end of Ex. 8 and later in a more complex manner, often gives the work a distinctly Balinese feel, as, of course, does the emphasis on metal sonorities. It is even possible that McPhee's practice of notating ostinatos as repeating number sequences sparked off the 4:3:2:3:4 structure of the Cage piece, with the numbers now interpreted not as pitches but as lengths of time.

However, when Cage himself came to speak of his structural methods, in a lecture given in 1948, he named his models as Webern and Satie, who, he claimed, had been responsible for the 'one new idea since Beethoven' in the field of musical structure. His reasoning as to why this 'one new idea' should be preferred is disarmingly simple. Sound and silence, he points out, have only one quality in common, that of duration, and so it follows that duration is fundamental: 'There can be no right making of music', he insists, 'that does not structure itself from the very roots of sound and silence – lengths of time.' And as witness for the defence he calls Webern's Op. 11 (a rather dubious example) and, much more plausibly, Satie's *Choses vues à droite et à gauche*, in which he points out, among other things, that the 'Fantasie musculaire' is a play on units of two, three, and four bars.

The advantage of structuring music by lengths of time rather than by some harmonic system – an advantage already foreseen in the manifesto of 1937 – is not only that silence can be treated according to the same rules as sound but also that those rules can be applied indifferently to pitched sounds and to noises, as they are in the *First Construction*. Previously Cage had pursued his belief in the equality of noises with pitched sounds by using similar principles for each in separate pieces (e.g. the Trio for percussion and the Three Pieces for flutes, both of 1935), but now he could deal with both together, and indeed *Imaginary Landscape No. 1* and the *First Construction* were the first pieces in which he used unpitched (or indefinitely pitched) and pitched sounds together. At the same time he had discovered a method which took over a large part of the decision-making of musical composition, a method which therefore facilitated objective creation and which could also be used by others. Even in 1937 this had been one of his implied aims; in 1948 it was to be stated plainly, for Cage concludes by affirming: 'The function of a piece of music is to bring into co-being elements paradoxical by nature, to bring into one situation elements that can be and ought to be agreed upon – that is, Law elements – together with elements that cannot and ought not to be agreed upon – that is, Freedom elements.'

In the terms of this lecture, which defines four basic aspects of a musical composition, the *First Construction* exhibits the application of law to structure (the 16^2 division of time), material (the sixteen rhythmic patterns, the sixteen sounds in each voice), and method (the formation of a six-part counterpoint of different rhythmic layers). The only freedom is in the form, by which Cage, using the word in an unusual sense, understands 'the morphological line of the sound-continuity' and which, with a welcome change of terminology, he later opposes to structure ('mind-controlled') as belonging to the heart. In other words, with a fixed framework, fixed materials, and fixed ways of working, Cage allowed himself freedom in how he placed events within the durational grid.

Few of his later works enforce the law of rhythmic structure with the same rigour, and few show the same constriction on materials and methods, but the idea of integrating law and structure with form and freedom was to remain fundamental until the early 1950s. The *Second Construction* for percussion quartet (1940), which quickly followed the first, has a similar structure of 16^2 bars, but now with the internal proportions 4:3:4:5. These time-lengths are very clear in the first sixteen-bar section, where the two four-bar units are occupied by a sleigh-bells solo and the others by a tam-tam, but the final six sections are taken up by a 'fugue' on a rhythmic theme related to that of the initial sleigh-bells solo, and the rhythmic structure is forgotten. In the *Third Construction* (1941), also for percussion quartet, the structure of 24^2 bars is evident but the internal divisions of the sections show no regularity. This was to be the pattern of the future. The division into sections is generally marked in the score by double barlines, but the music may often go against these divisions and against the proportions within them.

The *Third Construction* was written for a San Francisco percussion ensemble which Cage led with Lou Harrison, as was the *Double Music* (1941) on which they collaborated, demonstrating that Cage truly had devised a method which could be 'agreed upon'. Two of the four parts are by Harrison, these being composed in units of nine-and-a-half bars; the other two are by Cage, who counteracts Harrison's scheme with one built in sections of seven or fourteen bars (part 3) and with a freely written solo (part 1). The ensemble had available a wide variety of instruments, both eastern and western, pitched and unpitched, conventional and home-made, but they came more and more to concentrate on found and invented objects, such as the sets of five graduated tin cans that figure prominently in the *Third Construction*. And in *Living Room Music* (1940) Cage provided his four players with purely rhythmic parts which may be interpreted on 'any household or architectural elements', including books, magazines, items of furniture, and walls. The suite also includes a movement for speech quartet in which a typically banal sentence by Gertrude Stein – 'Once upon a time the world was round and you could go on it around and around' – is rhythmically enunciated within a structure of 7^2 bars.

A willingness to use assorted objects as musical instruments was not unusual among adventurous American composers at this time: Henry Brant was probably the pioneer with his *Music for a Five and Dime Store* of 1931. Cage, however, was influenced as much by Duchamp's practice of making unconsidered artefacts into works of art, and he does seem to have been the first to insert miscellaneous pieces of wood, cardboard, rubber, or metal between the strings of a piano, altering the sounds profoundly and effectively making the instrument into a one-man percussion ensemble. The date of his first 'prepared piano' is, however, uncertain. His earliest solo for the instrument was unquestionably *Bacchanale*, for which many sources give the date 1938 but which is dated 'March 1940' in the score. Cage himself believes the later date to be more likely, in which case the prepared piano was born two months earlier, albeit in rudimentary form, in the *Second Construction*, where the 'string piano' has a screw and a piece of cardboard inserted into it. *Bacchanale*, however, goes further than this, requiring the 'muting' of all the twelve notes used in the piece. The materials needed for the preparation comprise one small bolt, one screw with nuts, and eleven pieces of fibrous weather stripping, and their positioning and sizes are to be determined by experiment.

The novelty of the prepared piano was not only that it placed a variety of percussion sounds beneath the pianist's fingers, but also that it allowed the composer, and to a lesser extent the performer, to choose sounds empirically. Instead of writing for the more or less defined timbres of standard instruments, the composer could try out various objects at various points in the piano, working in the manner more of an electronic composer than of an orchestrator. The corresponding disadvantage is that the sounds cannot be stipulated with any exactitude. Even when Cage gives precise measurements for the positioning of the preparations, as he does in most of his later works for prepared piano, the resulting sounds still depend a great deal on the instrument's build: comparing recordings of the same piece readily shows how markedly different the prepared pitches and timbres can be. What is even more disconcerting, however, is the oblique relationship between sound and score. On the printed page such a piece as *Bacchanale* looks like ordinary piano music:

Ex. 9

But of course the sounds are not what the symbols lead one to expect: the pitches may well be changed, and the notes will have gained the thud or metallic clang of percussion instruments, making *Bacchanale* even more Balinese than it looks. The whole meaning of notation is thus changed. No longer is it an accurate representation of sound but only a system of instructions to the performer, and this revolution was to have important consequences later in Cage's career.

Bacchanale was also new in being the first of his compositions created specifically for a dance, choreographed by Syvilla Fort. During the next few years Cage created many more short dance scores for prepared piano, and in 1942 he began an association with the choreographer Merce Cunningham: their first work together was *Credo in Us*, scored for a percussion quartet in which one part is for gramophone or radio. This time, by contrast with *Imaginary Landscape No. 1*, Cage uses not abstract sound effects but prefabricated material, in that the radio introduces whatever happens to be on the air at the time (though the player is wisely advised to 'avoid News programs during national or international emergencies') and the gramophone plays 'some classic: e.g. Dvořák, Beethoven, Sibelius, or Shostakovich'. The choice, dictated here by what was most highly regarded in the symphonic repertory of 1942, is not as important as the sense of dislocation when the 'classic' is subjected to the chops of Cage's rhythmic structure, as well as to the heedless additions of his poverty-stricken percussion (tin cans are again prominent, with an electric buzzer) and his often jazz-tinged piano. The only commercial recording (EMI Electrola 1 C 165-28954/7 Y) aptly chooses Dvořák's Ninth Symphony to suffer this indignity, underlining the fact that now the new world can blithely assert its total independence from the old, without even the connection of malicious ridicule.

Shortly before the composition of *Credo in Us* Cage had the opportunity to work in a Chicago radio station and there to create two further pieces in the *Imaginary Landscape* series of electronic forays. The second in the cycle is basically a percussion piece, flourishing a virtuoso tin-can solo and having one player use a coil of wire attached to a gramophone cartridge and amplified, but the third has a much greater variety of electronic effects: a buzzer, an oscillator, three turntables playing frequency recordings and generator whine, a 'marimbula' with a contact microphone, and again an amplified coil of wire. Unlike the tentative *Imaginary Landscape No. 1*, this is real performance music for electronic devices, and in an article written soon after its composition Cage speculated about the possibility of giving concerts 'in the midst of a fantastic assemblage of wires and electrical connections'. That, however, was still some way off, and *Imaginary Landscape No. 3* was to have no successor until Cage's methods had changed considerably.

Instead his remaining works of the 1940s were divided into two categories: ballet scores, mostly for prepared piano, and concert music, consisting in the main of sets of instrumental pieces. In his concert pieces, and in the *Imaginary Landscapes*, he continued to use the rhythmic-structure principle of the *First Construction*, while the dance scores were usually composed according to irregular rhythmic structures dictated by the choreography, though in *Tossed as it is Untroubled* (1943) this situation was reversed and Cunningham devised a dance to follow Cage's structure of 7^2 bars.

Very little of Cage's music from this period is vocal. The Cummings songs of 1938 were followed only by another Cummings setting, *Forever and Sunsmell* for voice and percussion duo (1942), a dance score for Cunningham's colleague Jean Erdman, by *The Wonderful Widow of Eighteen Springs* for voice and closed piano (also 1942), by the textless Duet for voice and prepared piano from the unfinished concert programme *She is Asleep* (1943), and by *Experiences No. 2* for voice alone (1948), which was based on an earlier Cunningham score for piano duo. Yet these works, as much as the larger bulk of music for prepared piano, demonstrate Cage's openness, both in freely allowing transposition of his vocal lines and in discovering, in the case of *The Wonderful Widow*, a whole new instrument in the woodwork of the grand piano. The vocal pieces also demonstrate how much he could achieve with extremely limited resources, for they all look back to 'In just Spring' in making do with a very few notes. *The Wonderful Widow*, for example, has just three, a chanting note together with the major second below and the fourth above, and of course there are no defined pitches in the rhythmically active part for closed piano, whose notation indicates which part of the instrument is to be struck and with what (fingers or, in the case of cross-headed notes, knuckles):

Ex. 10

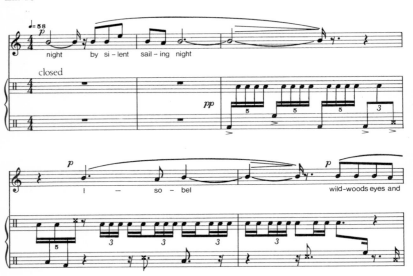

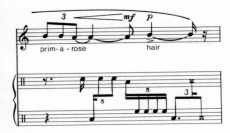

prim-a-rose   hair

Cage was also using only a very small repertory of sounds in his pieces for percussion ensemble and for prepared piano. Among the latter, *Tossed as it is Untroubled* and *Root of an Unfocus*, for instance, need just eight prepared notes, and the tiny *Prelude for Meditation* has only four. But when this technique was transferred to a pitched instrument, the voice, it necessarily brought with it a feeling of modality, and Cage seems to have been stimulated to explore modal composition further, though the influence of Satie must also have played a part. Pentatonic modes are employed in the two versions of *Experiences* and in other works, including the first movement of the Suite for Toy Piano (1948), which shows Cage's self-denial in the field of pitch at its most extreme:

Ex. 11

The whole five-movement work uses only nine different pitches in the Phrygian mode.

Less confined is *In a Landscape* for piano or harp (also 1948), which at its beginning shows very clearly the importance of Satie:

Ex. 12

In terms of repetitiveness, however, this work is far outdone by *Music for Marcel Duchamp* for prepared piano (1947), which ends with seven slow statements of the same winding four-bar unit:

Ex. 13

This is also an extreme instance of Cage's disguising his rhythmic structure, for the music utterly ignores the marked units of eleven bars, and does so with a flat purposelessness that was gaining ground in Cage's output in the later 1940s. He had begun this period, in such works as the *First Construction* and *Bacchanale*, by filling his pre-arranged time schemes with dynamism, but now there was a tendency to leave a vacuum of silence or of empty repetition. It was as if he was intentionally showing up the passive nature of his rhythmic-structure technique, which asks for time simply to be filled and not necessarily engaged: where earlier his ostinatos had made the technique work in an active manner, now he was sometimes content to let his ideas loose in music having no such directing impulse.

However, the 1940s also saw some of Cage's most dynamic and most fully elaborated works, among them a sequence of big concert works for the prepared piano: the six-movement suite *The Perilous Night* (1943-4), the duo collections *A Book of Music* (1944), and Three Dances (1944-5), and the seventy-minute Sonatas and Interludes (1946-8). All of these show a changed approach to the instrument which Cage had invented, for the vague instructions and the few preparations of *Bacchanale* are replaced by precise indications for the location of a great many objects, with thirty-six notes altered in each piano for the Three Dances and forty-five for the Sonatas and Interludes. The preparation in all four works affects the bass most severely, since there rubber and plastic materials are used to generate thuds and rattles, whereas the treble is generally prepared with screws and bolts, which add a gamelan-like shimmer but keep a sense of pitch, even if the pitch is changed. The Sonatas and Interludes are unusual in using some unprepared notes, as in the Second Interlude, where there is a play between prepared and unprepared F♯s, but even where all the notes are prepared the insistent repetitions maintain the feeling of modality.

A special feature of the two duo works is the operation of a single system of durational proportions throughout, with the introduction of a subtle ploy to relate changes of tempo to changes of proportional system so that the rhythmic structure is preserved in clock time. For example, the first of the Three Dances is constructed in thirty-bar units of 2/2 bars at minim = 88, the second in thirty-nine-bar units with the same time signature but at a tempo of minim = 114 (though the effect is of a slower tempo because the prevailing quaver durations of the first dance are replaced by crotchets), and the third in fifty-seven-bar units with again the same 2/2 metre but with the tempo further increased to minim = 168 (and here the quaver pulse returns in a relentless *moto perpetuo*). Thus the changing lengths are almost exactly counterbalanced by the changing tempos so that the units in all the dances have the same duration of approximately forty-one seconds. And in *A Book of Music* there are four similarly interlocked tempos governing a set of twelve pieces.

The volume of Sonatas and Interludes is also a set of small pieces, sixteen sonatas grouped in quartets and separated by four interludes, but now there is only the shadow of a general rhythmic structure: for example, the sonatas of the last quartet all have four hundred bars and the middle two of that quartet, XIV and XV, have the same internal proportions, the same tempo, and even many identical motifs (they are named as a pair, 'Gemini'). Within the sonatas the rhythmic structures are much more evident, each having a bipartite form with repetitions to embody a system of proportions at two levels. For example, Sonata XIII is divided into sections of 40:20 (repeated) and 40:40:40:20 (repeated) crotchets, so that it expresses the proportions 2:1:2:1:2:2:2:1:2:2:2:1. And the choice of 20 as factor makes it possible for the first section itself to unfold, though with some disguise, the same rhythmic structure (in the following example asterisks have been placed over the notes which are not prepared):

Ex. 14

The simplicity of Sonata XIII is not typical of the set, and in most cases the reproduction of the rhythmic structure within sections has to be taken largely on trust. This movement is, however, typical in showing greater freedom in the fields of pitch and timbre than in that of rhythm. According to Cage's own account, his method was that of 'considered improvisation' and he chose the preparations 'as one chooses shells while walking along a beach'.

With the Sonatas and Interludes the prepared piano, originally a scratch construction, had become an instrument of great sophistication, and the rhythmic-structure technique had been developed to a high point of finesse. Cage was in danger of creating a masterpiece, and perhaps for this very reason he broke off composition for a while. After finishing the Sonatas and Interludes he wrote two dance scores, *Dream* and *In a Landscape*, and also the Suite for Toy Piano, but then there was nothing for nearly a year until he began work on his String Quartet (1949–50). His attitudes and methods were changing again, and in an easterly direction already foreshadowed in some of the works of the 1940s. First there had been *Amores* for prepared piano and percussion trio (1943), where 'an attempt was made', he has said, 'to express in combination the erotic and the tranquil, two of the permanent emotions of Indian tradition'. The Sonatas and Interludes go further in the expression of these 'permanent emotions', fixing 'the heroic, the erotic, the wondrous, the mirthful, sorrow, fear, anger, the odious, and their common tendency towards tranquility', though it would certainly be a mistake to attempt to assign these eight states severally to the sixteen sonatas: what stands out is the 'common tendency'. Then in his first orchestral work, the ballet *The Seasons* (1947), he had looked to Indian associations of winter with quiescence, spring with creation, summer with preservation, and autumn with destruction, and this he was to do again in the String Quartet. But by then the eastern influence was to be much more than merely poetic.

TOWARDS SILENCE

IN 1949 Cage visited Paris, and gave there a performance of the Sonatas and Interludes which won the interest and admiration of Pierre Boulez. The two composers struck up a close friendship, and when Cage returned to New York, with his new String Quartet half completed, it was with the benefit of Boulez's latest ideas for the furthering of serialism. However, he had already embarked on a course very different from that of his colleague.

The full title of the quartet, 'String Quartet in Four Parts', is not a tautology, for in fact the instruments are treated not at all as independent voices but rather as components in a single sound-producing ensemble: the 'parts' are the four seasonal movements. As in certain preceding works, including *The Seasons*, Cage uses what he calls a 'gamut' of prescribed pitches and chords, this in imitation of the fixed repertory of sounds produced by the prepared piano. But in the String Quartet the gamut is much narrower than hitherto and the rhythmic variety is drastically reduced. The removal of incident reaches an extreme in the winter slow movement, marked 'Nearly stationary', where the same chords keep returning, always on one or other of the two minim beats:

Ex. 15

The monotone effect is heightened throughout the work by the absence of vibrato and the relatively high density of harmonics, as well as by the consistent limitation of each note to a particular string, so that even the frequent F major triads are whitened into austerity.

Clearly the quartet had stylistic roots in Satie, but it was also deeply influenced by Cage's recent studies of mystical thought. In an article of 1949 he quotes Meister Eckhart to the effect that: 'The soul itself is so simple that it cannot have more than one idea at a time of anything.'

Hence his abnegation in the quartet and succeeding works of any counterpoint. In the same short essay he makes statements which testify to the importance of his studies of Zen Buddhism under Daisetz T. Suzuki at Columbia University, statements such as: 'The responsibility of the artist consists in perfecting his work so that it may become attractively disinteresting.' The composer, and by implication the listener, was to remain 'innocent and free to receive anew with each Now-moment a heavenly gift' (another quotation from Meister Eckhart), and preserving that innocence and freedom meant renouncing anything which might encourage the mind to acts of relation or memory: the musical processes had to be purposeless, and in the quartet Cage, like Satie, achieved that largely by repetition.

He used the same style in the Six Melodies for violin and piano (1950) but then produced something of a throwback to the world of *The Wonderful Widow* in *A Flower* for voice and closed piano (also 1950). This work is, however, unique in having a double rhythmic structure of 7^2 bars of $5/4$ superimposed on 5^2 bars of $10/4$, a refinement suggesting that the old proportional principle had reached its period of decadence. It was, however, to remain in operation in the works of the next few years, and nowhere more obviously than in the Concerto for prepared piano and chamber orchestra, which was begun in the same year of 1950.

The concerto is at once an apotheosis of Cage's earlier style, with its solo part for an instrument having fifty-three prepared notes, and a further step in the direction pointed by the quartet. Learning from Boulez, Cage places his musical elements in squared charts, but not with the intention of generating a serial construction: instead the charts are an aid to the objective deployment of a gamut of pitches, chords, and noises. The chamber orchestra is a colourful assembly of twenty-two soloists, and so there is a much greater variety of sounds than in the String Quartet, with the percussion benefiting from the *Construction* and *Imaginary Landscape* series in their use of unconventional instruments and electrical devices. But the sparseness and Eckhartian singleness of the events is the same as in the quartet, and so too is the tempo. Ex. 16 shows the very beginning of the work, where, as throughout, entries are nearly always on one of the four crotchets in each bar:

Ex. 16

The pointillist texture suggests comparison with contemporary
European works, such as Boulez's *Polyphonie X* and Stockhausen's
Spiel, but the rhythmic poverty and the frequent pitch repetitions
create an aimlessness quite peculiar to Cage.

The concerto has three parts, or movements, which are played without interruption and which, as in the String Quartet, map out the rhythmic structure (in this case 3:2:4:4:2:3:5; cf. Ex. 16) on the largest scale, having nine, nine, and five sections. In the first part, Cage has said, he 'let the pianist express the opinion that music should be improvised or felt, while the orchestra expressed only the chart, with no personal taste involved'. The second part brings both pianist and orchestra under the rule of the chart, and the third locks both together in a single set of 'moves'. Yet the most striking feature of this final part is bound to be its approach to silence, for not only is the texture thinned down but large elements of the structure, including the final five bars of each section, are empty of notation. Such oddities as this wildly virtuoso bar:

Ex. 17

are bizarre bursts of activity in music marching slowly towards extinction, and apart from them the landscape is bleak indeed. 'Until that time', Cage has recalled, 'my music had been based on the idea that you had to say something. The charts gave me my first indication of the possibility of saying nothing.'

The charts also showed Cage how music could be made purposeless without being repetitive in the manner of the String Quartet: events simply had to be left to follow one another without meaningful relation, as they are again in the Sixteen Dances for nonet (1951) which followed the concerto. But if subjective decisions were to be removed entirely, there had to be some impersonal means of choosing material and of proceeding on the chart. These means were soon found. The radio, already used in *Credo in Us*, presented itself as a source of unpredictable sounds, and the chart 'moves' could be made randomly with the help of the *I Ching*, or Chinese book of changes, originally a guide for obtaining oracular messages from the fall of a group of yarrow sticks: hence *Imaginary Landscape No. 4* for twelve radios (1951), for which coin tosses decided frequencies of tuning, dynamics, durations, tempos, and numbers of superimposed events. The irony of such labour being expended on randomness is necessarily heightened by the nature of the work, for the scrupulously notated score, with its markings of frequencies and volume levels, will obviously produce very different results depending on the time and place of performance. At the première the start was delayed and so, as Cowell reported, the radios 'were unable to capture programs diversified enough to present a really interesting specific result'. But Cage was not concerned with interesting or with a 'specific result', rather with making a 'musical composition the continuity of which is free of individual taste and memory (psychology) and also of the literature and "traditions" of the art'. 'Value judgements', he continued, 'are not in the nature of this work as regards either composition, performance, or listening. The idea of relation (the idea: 2) being absent, anything (the idea: 1) may happen. A "mistake" is beside the point, for once anything happens it authentically is.'

The same methods and the same Zen principles lie behind the *Music of Changes*, whose composition immediately followed that of *Imaginary Landscape No. 4* and in which the radio frequencies are replaced by notes, chords, clusters, and some noises to be played on a piano. Lasting for forty-three minutes, this is one of the most demanding scores in the repertory, as may be suggested by a short extract:

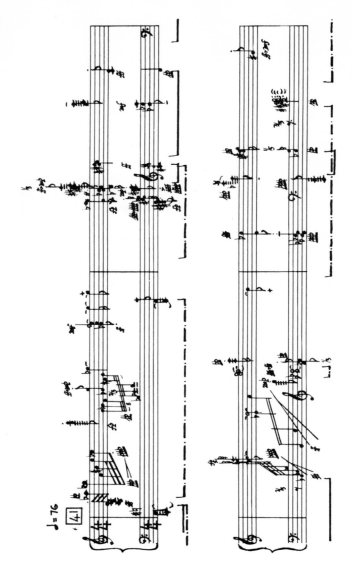

The fractions indicate irrational durations as parts of a crotchet, and the sound events and rests thrown up by the chance procedures are laid out according to a space-time notation whereby each 4/4 bar occupies ten centimetres. Sometimes, as in the second bar of Ex. 18, the coin tosses ask for impractical combinations: 'In such instances', Cage notes, 'the performer is to employ his own discretion.'

With *Imaginary Landscape No. 4* and the *Music of Changes* Cage might have seemed to have achieved his goal of letting sounds 'be themselves', 'unimpeded by service to any abstraction', so that the work was, in the Zen spirit, a vehicle not of thoughts but only of events. The proportional duration structures hark back to earlier compositions, but the sounds are all dictated by chance, and Cage kept to this method of using chance procedures to fill an empty time canvas in the *Two Pastorales* (1951-2), which are much simpler than the *Music of Changes* but which introduce some preparations and, in the second piece, 'accessory instruments' in the shape of two whistles: such additions to the pianist's technical repertory were to be developed in works of the next few years. The space-time notation of the *Pastorales* and their immediate predecessors points at Cage's awareness of tape, where similarly duration is represented by length, and during the same period he produced two tape pieces: *Imaginary Landscape No. 5* and *Williams Mix* (both 1952). These are, however, as open as the radio work, for both are presented as detailed scores for the preparation of tapes from snippets, using any forty-two gramophone records in the case of *Imaginary Landscape No. 5* and, for *Williams Mix*, a variety of sounds in six categories: 'city sounds', 'country sounds', 'electronic sounds', 'manually produced sounds, including the literature of music', 'wind-produced sounds, including songs', and 'small sounds requiring amplification to be heard with the others'. Thus while most composers were using the new medium as a means for the total determination of a work, Cage was finding in it a way to create the most diverse and undefined collages, another route to ridding music of personal taste and of consequence.

As Cage has often acknowledged, his break into chance procedures in 1951-2 was helped by the new associates he gained after his visit to Paris. The *Music of Changes* could not have been conceived except for the dexterous fingers of David Tudor, who was to remain a close collaborator for many years, and Cage also found support in a group of fellow composers (Morton Feldman, Earle Brown, Christian Wolff) and painters (Jasper Johns, Robert Rauschenberg). Several of these men were present with Cage in the summer of 1952 at Black Mountain

College in North Carolina, where four years earlier Cage had written the Suite for Toy Piano and where now there was conceived the first of those unstructured performances later known as 'happenings': something of the same spirit entered Cage's *Water Music* for pianist (also 1952), where a poster-size score, intended to be seen by the audience, asks the player to engage in a whole range of activities beyond the keyboard (blowing whistles, pouring water, using a radio, and so on). Then, on 29 August 1952 in Woodstock, New York, Tudor gave the first performance of a new Cage work billed as *4′ 33″*. He came on to the stage, made as if to play, but produced no sound in any of the three movements lasting together for the title duration (in fact the piece can be performed for any length of time, taking its title from that chosen). Silence had been reached, and the authority of the composer extinguished.

BEYOND COMPOSING

CAGE has said, and often repeated, that 'the music I prefer, even to my own or anybody else's, is what we are hearing if we are just quiet'. *4′ 33″* was thus not just a comic stunt but a demonstration that the sounds of the environment have a value no less than that of composed music, for in truth there is no silence, whether here or in the empty spaces of *Music for Marcel Duchamp* and the Concerto for prepared piano. Even in an anechoic chamber, Cage discovered, one is assailed by the sounds of one's own body; anywhere else it is impossible to escape the sounds of men, machines, animals, wind, or whatever. Generally such sounds are regarded as interruptions to music, but for Cage, seeking an art of non-intention, they provided the perfect unforeseeable material, and all of his later works must be regarded as taking place concurrently with *4′ 33″*: chance-composed itself, the music is hospitable to the chance eventuality.

After *4′ 33″* Cage set about winning for performers the same freedom he had achieved for sounds in the works of 1951–2. By 1958 he had decided that the *Music of Changes* 'is an object more inhuman than human', because 'these things that constitute it, though only sounds, have come together to control a human being'. If human beings were not to be so controlled, notation had to be more open, and Cage curiously found his way to innovation here through writing for the carillon. He noted that it was very difficult to limit the duration of a carillon tone, and so in *Music for Carillon No. 1* (1952) he simply omitted to notate durations. His compositional method, too, was simpler. Instead of going through lengthy routines of coin tossing he folded scraps of paper, cut holes at points of folding, and then used the scraps as stencils on squared paper to produce a graph score in the manner of Feldman:

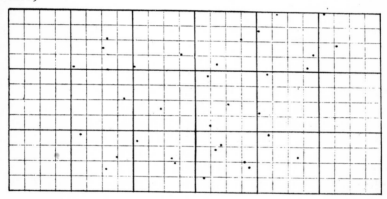

Time is marked out by the vertical lines in quarter seconds and pitch by the horizontal lines; the published realizations convert the dots into uniform semibreves so that points of attack are indicated but not durations.

This same kind of notation was used in the *Music for Piano* series (1952-6), a cycle of four separate pieces (1, 2, 3, and 20) and five batches of sixteen (4-19, 21-36, 37-52, 53-68, 69-84). Cage used the *I Ching* to determine how many sounds there should be per page (with the exception of the first two, each piece is confined to one page); he then placed the sounds according to where there were imperfections in his paper. The layout, with notes scattered at random across the page, may suggest that some sounds will be sustained for longer than others, but the tempo is in each case free, as are the dynamics (except in 1). In

Music for Piano 1 Cage invites the performer to interpret the music with a variety of keyboard and inside-piano techniques, but in later pieces he specifies which notes are to be muted ('M') or played pizzicato ('P'), and from *Music for Piano 21* onwards he includes noises made on the woodwork (notated on a central line). The following extract from *Music for Piano 68* shows events of all kinds:

Ex. 20

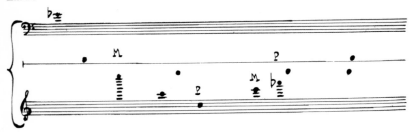

A further matter of variability in the *Music for Piano* series is the programming of the pieces. Cage allows that the sets of sixteen may be given as solo items or combined in any way by any number of pianists, so that the identity of each piece, which is already sketchy given the liberties in timing and volume, can be more or less obliterated in performances of greater or lesser density.

The same holds true of Cage's other major effort of the early 1950s, the set of pieces with time-length titles, which in respect of notational complexity contrast markedly with the *Music for Piano* series. The set began with six short works for string player composed in the summer of 1953, of which *59½″* was published separately and the remaining five pieces were incorporated within a larger work, *26′ 1.1499″*, in 1955. Other members of the constellation are *34′ 46.776″* and *31′57.9864″*, both written in 1954 for solo pianist, and *27′ 10.554″* for percussionist (1956). Segments from the four half-hour works can be combined together in any manner by any number of players, with or without parts of the lecture '45′ for a Speaker' (1954). Thus the closely defined material is laid open to the chance occurrences of undefined forms in a way that looked forward to Boulez's Third Piano Sonata and Stockhausen's *Klavierstück XI*. Indeed, there was opportunity for direct influence, for *34′ 46.776″* and *31′ 57.9864″* were written for Cage and Tudor to play as a duo at the 1954 Donaueschingen Festival during the composer's first visit to Europe since 1949.

Music for Piano and the time-length pieces can be regarded as obverses in their approach to non-intention: in the former the notation is so vague that the composer's scope is greatly reduced, whereas in the latter it is so demanding that the performer has little opportunity to overlay his own intentions. In the case of the two piano volumes the customary staff notation, with durations represented by distances according to a marked sliding scale, is joined by three bands indicating, from top to bottom, the force of attack (most at the top), its distance (furthest at the top), and its speed (slowest at the top):

Ex. 21

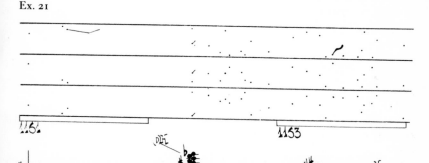

Even without such refinements the music would be difficult enough, as this excerpt from *34′ 46.776″* shows. The large group occupies approximately a second-and-a-half, within which time the performer must play two notes on the strings ('H') and move the object used to prepare the A♯ between the two appearances of that note. Cage also requires in both time-length piano works the use of accessory instruments, adding to the powerful impression given by these pieces of performance as action, of music as abstract theatrical gesture: that, too, was to impress the composer's European colleagues.

The method of *34′ 46.776″* and *31′ 57.9864″*, involving *I Ching* operations and the observation of paper imperfections, was also that of the string and percussion pieces, though the latter are differently notated. The string player is confronted with a graphic score showing the finger position on each of the strings and also the bowing pressure, besides which Cage stipulates the bowing, the position of the bow, the part of the bow used, and the kinds of pizzicato and vibrato required. Moreover, like the pianists with their accessory instruments, the player has the opportunity to introduce 'other sounds', which 'may issue from entirely other sources, e.g. percussion instruments, whistles, radios, etc.' *27′ 10.554″* may appear less demanding, since the notation shows only the timing and loudness (distance above or below the medial line representing *mf*) of sounds from instruments in four categories: metal, wood, skin, and 'all others, e.g. electronic devices, mechanical arrangements, radios, whistles, etc':

Ex. 22

However, the density of events and the expected multiplicity of instruments, including the usual *Imaginary Landscape* innovations, would suggest a performance of extreme virtuosity.

Thus the time-length pieces appear to control their performers quite as completely as had the *Music of Changes*. But there is an important difference. In his introductory remarks to the piano works Cage allows that 'the notation may be read in any "focus" (as many or as few of its aspects being acted upon)', and so with elegant economy he changes the meaning of the score. It becomes an invitation to perform at the limits of technique, a prescription for action (as had been the case with the works for prepared piano) and not the representation of an ideal. Indeed, the titles themselves point at the absurdity of the notion of an ideal performance, with their prescriptions of timing to a ten-thousandth of a second, even though these timings have their place in what was Cage's last use of proportional schemes of duration. So the performer is liberated just as much as he is in the *Music for*

Piano series, and perhaps more so, for he has the opportunity to choose his own instruments, wholly in the case of *27′ 10.554″* and partly in the companion works.

It seems that more pieces in this series were planned, but instead Cage went on to create another work for a number of uncoordinated solos, the *Concert for Piano and Orchestra* (1957–8), where there are parts for piano and thirteen other instruments, to which may be added two *Solos for Voice* (1958–60) and other pieces. Performers are free to use any of this material in any combination, so that at one limit the *Concert* can be a repetition of *4′ 33″* and at the other a mix of musical activity. The work is thus a widely adaptable store of music, and it is a similarly diverse treasury of notational innovations. Among the multitude of events scattered across the sixty-four pages of the piano solo Cage distinguishes eighty-four varieties of compositional technique, each giving rise to a more or less distinctive graphic style. There is room for the techniques of *Music for Piano* and *34′ 46.776″*, and also, in the case of noises, *27′ 10.554″*; there are fragments which might have strayed from the more recent *Winter Music* (1957), a loose liaison of chords spaced out on twenty pages like star cracks on ice. At the same time there are notations which depart much further from convention, whether to ask for new playing techniques or to make an unusual degree of choice available to the player.

Ex. 23, from p. 12, is characteristic of the bulk of the *Concert* piano solo in using some traditional symbols together with new features which specify (or fail to specify) unconventional elements:

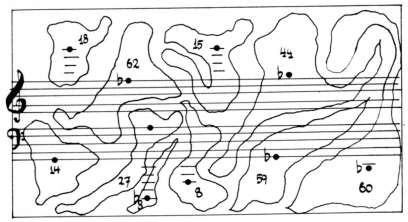

In this case each 'island' represents a cluster which changes in register during time according to the shape outlined, and which is centred on the marked pitch. The numbers refer to a scale of loudness from 1 to 64, which may be interpreted by the performer as going from soft to loud or from loud to soft. Ex. 24, from p. 54, shows a rather stranger notational device, where the points indicate positions where sounds are to be produced:

Ex. 24

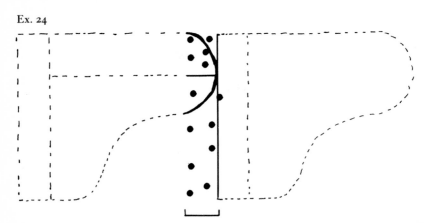

Clearly there is the possibility of one keyboard sound, as well as several on the woodwork of the instrument, but others invite the player to use his own resources. In terms of graphic extraordinariness, however,

34

there are few rivals for Ex. 25, from p. 57, where the four meandering lines represent frequency, duration, amplitude, and overtone structure in any correspondence:

Ex. 25

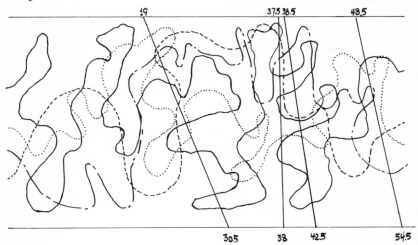

The performer is required to draw perpendiculars from either the upper or the lower horizontal line to the slanting lines. Measurements from the base line to the points of intersection with the wavy lines are then used to determine values for the four parameters according to scales determined by the player. The numbers in the diagram show by their differences the time available for sounds derived from references to each of the slanting lines: 11.5 seconds in the case of the first, for example.

These three illustrations, though diverse, can give no more than a hint of the notational virtuosity of the *Concert* and of the manifold ways in which Cage makes the performer a co-creator who must work out his own realizations of the instructions given (as in the case of Ex. 25), who must command a whole range of new techniques, and who is at liberty, as in *34′ 46.776″* and *31′ 57.9864″*, to introduce ancillary instruments of his own choice. The *Concert* piano solo had its offshoots in *For Paul Taylor and Anita Dencks* (1957) and *TV Köln* (1958), each of which uses just one of the eighty-four compositional methods, but its more important successor, composed while the *Concert* was in progress and also using one of its strategies, was

Variations I (1958). This work was dedicated to Tudor, for whom the piano solo of the *Concert* was written, but for the first time the score is not so limited, being available to 'any number of performers; any kind or number of instruments'.

Such versatility was possible because here Cage dispenses with all notational specifics. The abundant devices of the *Concert* are replaced by a single square bearing a random scatter of black points, on which may be placed any one of five transparent squares, each inscribed with five straight lines. Rather as in Ex. 25, perpendiculars are dropped from the points to the lines to give measurements for the five variables of frequency, overtone structure, amplitude, duration, and attack point. In this simple way Cage had chanced on the means to make no preconditions while also providing, as he had refrained from doing in the equally versatile *4′ 33″*, an aid to performers in the production of sound. He has himself demonstrated the abundant possibilities of such a score in the case of *Fontana Mix* (also 1958), whose notational principles are based on those of Ex. 25 but which again uses transparent sheets to allow various configurations of the designs, readings from which were employed in the composition of a tape collage with the title *Fontana Mix* (1958-9), an *Aria* for solo voice (1958), the *Water Walk* for solo television performance (1959), and the *Theatre Piece* for up to eight performers (1960).

Cage's removal of his intentions in *Variations I* and *Fontana Mix*, as also in his continuing use of radios as sources of material (*Speech*, 1955; *Radio Music*, 1956), must be understood in the light of his consistent commitment to a Zen music of purposelessness and absence of thought. He begins from the premise that if art is to be useful (a favourite term of commendation) it must not be separate from life. The artist is to alert his audience to the beauties of everyday life, not substitute some beauty of his own, and he can best do this if he takes as his guide the unwilled creative processes in the world, if he 'imitates nature in her manner of operation' (a cherished thought Cage drew from Ananda K. Coomaraswamy). Cage himself has usually chosen to imitate nature's more random phenomena: his special interest is in those organisms, fungi, which are most difficult to identify, most variable in form, most thoroughly interpenetrated with their surroundings, and he has likened the *Concert for Piano and Orchestra* to the experience of a forest or a city street, in both of which the observer may find extreme contrasts and a multitude of apparently meaningless events. Nor is this inclination towards the unpredictable and the unmeasured accidental, for Cage would wish that his music might be of assistance to people who must conduct themselves in a world so complex that much must seem haphazard. And it is important to note that he does not renounce this possibility of bringing about a mental change in his hearer, even while foreswearing particular musical intentions, which would, of course, call up a system of causality and hence stand in the way of the larger message.

The composer thus becomes a proposer, one who creates 'opportunities for experience' while denying himself those intentions of expressing, limiting, and shaping which Cage had willingly claimed in his works up to 1951. No less radically altered are the functions of performer and listener. One of Cage's dearest and most troublesome aims in the 1950s was to make musicians free without them becoming foolish, for though scores like *Variations I* are obviously invitations to anarchy, that anarchy need not be stupid or unconsidered. Indeed, faced with the opportunity to leave behind all restrictions of training and taste, the musician may find himself tested by a severe discipline, and Cage has repeatedly declared himself in favour of disciplined action as a road to music of Zero thought. His major undertakings of the 1950s were created not as complaisant exercises for amateurs but as invitations to Tudor to exploit the furthest limits of a formidable virtuoso technique, to discover the unpredicted and unpredictable. The listener, too, is challenged to attend with minute concentration, not relating what he hears to any previous experience but maintaining a state of unfettered receptiveness in which events may be tranquilly accepted. It may be objected that it is a small step from Zen no-mind to Dada mindlessness, from the mantra to the joke, but then even the Buddha smiles.

BEYOND MUSIC (AND BACK AGAIN)

THE year 1958, which began with *Variations I*, was one of the most eventful in Cage's career. It marked his silver jubilee as a composer (dating his output from the Sonata for clarinet), in celebration of which a concert was organized in New York to include the première of the *Concert for Piano and Orchestra*. It also saw the start of a long and highly successful tour of Europe, during which Cage was received with great interest at Darmstadt and given the opportunity to create new works in Stockholm (*Music Walk*), Cologne (*TV Köln*), and Milan (*Fontana Mix, Aria, Water Walk, Sounds of Venice*).

This new public prominence may have had a part in guiding him towards theatre, for several of these pieces, including most obviously the *Water Walk* which Cage devised for himself to perform on Italian television, take up from the absurd music theatre of *Water Music*. Then in 1960 came a tape project for a play by Jackson MacLow and Cage's own *Theatre Piece*, which invites each performer 'to prepare a thirty-minute program of action' suggested by 'a gamut of twenty nouns and/or verbs' of his own choosing. And part of the intention of *Cartridge Music* (also 1960) was to make electronic music theatrical, with players using objects inserted into gramophone cartridges, larger objects with contact microphones attached, and amplifiers.

However, Cage's involvement in theatre was also stimulated by his recognition, following his action music of the 1950s, that any separation of the musical from the theatrical is arbitrary, and by his new concerns. Where in the 1950s he had addressed his music to soloists and to individual listeners, he was now working very consciously in society: the widespread interest aroused by his first collection of essays, *Silence* (1961), may well have encouraged this. The pronouncements of Marshall McLuhan and Buckminster Fuller gained an importance in his mind at least equal to that of the dicta of mystics; he began to write a diary entitled 'How to Improve the World (You Will Only Make Matters Worse)' (1965-72); and he came to a view of art as 'giving instances of society suitable for social imitation – suitable because they show ways many centers can interpenetrate without obstructing one another, ways people can do things without being told or telling others what to do'.

Of course, all of Cage's music since 1952 had demonstrated his unwillingness to tell others what to do; what was new was his realization that music might have a role not only in changing ways of thinking but in altering society. His awareness of social change as a goal, however, led not to a larger but to a much reduced output, for between 1961 and 1969 he produced only a dozen or so projects, nearly all of them minimally dictatorial. Much the most fully notated work of this period is *Atlas eclipticalis* (1961–2), a collection of eighty-six instrumental parts to be played with or without electronic distortion. Like the *Concert for Piano and Orchestra* this is a set of independent solos, but the earlier work's profusion of compositional methods is replaced by just one: the derivation from star maps of delicate squiggles of notation, as in this extract from the fifth horn part:

Ex. 26

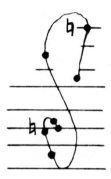

The work's further connection with the Zen non-intention of the 1950s is made very clear in the remarks which Cage made to the orchestra on the occasion of the first complete performance, in 1976, when he stated that the piece 'doesn't have any of my ideas or any of my feelings in it – it's just sounds'.

However, *Atlas eclipticalis* was a special case in being designed as a heavenly illustration of nirvana. When Cage came to complete his trilogy with works evoking samsara or 'the wheel of life' (*Variations IV*, 1963) and 'specific happening' (*4′ 33″ No. 2* or *0′ 0″*, 1962) his methods were quite different. *4′ 33″ No. 2* has one simple instruction – 'In a situation provided with maximum amplification (no feedback), perform a disciplined action' – and Cage coyly notes that its first performance was the writing of that sentence. *Variations IV* is a project for the production of sounds outside the place of performance, and its immersion in the world of everyday experience is pointed in the published recordings by the presence of a plethora of musical and radio events together with noises made by the audience. Furthermore, within the context of the *Variations* series, *Variations IV* marks a transfer from enigmatic diagrams to basic instructions for electronic audio-visual performances. *Variations II* (1961) is simply an economical abstract of *Variations I*, and *Variations III* (1962–3) is a similarly non-prescriptive kit which allows that 'any other activities are going on at the same time', as does *Variations IV*. *Variations V* (1965), however, is only a set of remarks written down after the first performance, which involved various kinds of electronic equipment, some of it responding in sound to the movements of dancers. One of these remarks notes the 'changed function of composer: to telephone, to raise money'.

But it was also the function of the composer to instigate helpful models of society. Electronics, as McLuhan was observing, had brought about a revolution in sensibility as profound as that ushered in by printing in the late fifteenth century, and Cage was responding to this not only by involving electronics in all his projects of this period (*Electronic Music for Piano* of 1964 is a cryptic note to Tudor on the subject, and the *Rozart Mix* of 1965 is an exchange of letters with Alvin Lucier arriving at a project for multiple tape loops) but also by devising performances which might make audiences aware of the nature of the revolution. In attending to the cornucopia of *Variations IV* the listener may find a way to enjoyment of the sensory abundance in the world, and in observing the transforming power of electronics in *Cartridge Music* he may realize how technological communication of a more utilitarian kind can nevertheless distort, whether maliciously or not. If Cage's works of the 1950s were concerned with an arousal to life, those of the 1960s were concerned more specifically with an arousal to life in a modern urban culture, where radio, television, and recordings can bring anyone in touch with events from throughout the world and with artefacts from throughout history. In an acknowledged refutation of the view of Meister Eckhart he had earlier approved, Cage noted: 'Nowadays everything happens at once and our souls are conveniently electronic (omniattentive).'

During the second half of the 1960s Cage concerned himself as an artist almost exclusively with jamborees for the electronic soul. *Variations VI* (1966) is a minimal set of instructions for several independent sound-systems, and the *Musicircus* of 1967 extended invitations to a whole host of performers providing fixed compositions, jazz music, a construction on which the audience could perform, lighting, large balloons, and refreshment stalls. There were also similar pluralities of events in *Reunion* (1968) and *HPSCHD* (1967–9), though the latter can be given more straightforwardly as music for harpsichords and tapes, a conjunction of Mozart, randomness, and computer-synthesized sound in a welter of complexity. The sunny optimism of these projects, though doubtless an expression of Cage's personality, was bolstered by Fuller's view that global resources would, thanks to technology, overtake demand, so that work would become obsolete, credit unlimited, hierarchies unnecessary.

But this sanguine view of an anarchist's utopia was not to be maintainable for long. The events of the late 1960s and early 1970s had their effect on Cage, who, while not abandoning his long-held aims for world improvement, appears to have concluded that more work would need to be done on an educational front, that collaboration had to be striven for and not merely assumed. Hence the initially surprising turnabout of his *Cheap Imitation* (1969), his first work in full traditional notation for more than a decade, though the stimulus for this piece came from circumstances beyond the composer's control. It happened that permission was not granted for Merce Cunningham to use a two-piano transcription by Cage of Satie's *Socrate*, and so Cage created a counterfeit of the melody, keeping the phrases rhythmically intact but choosing modes and notes in accordance with consultations of the *I Ching*. The following extracts show the openings of the Satie (Ex. 27a) and of the Cage (Ex. 27b):

Ex. 27

(a)

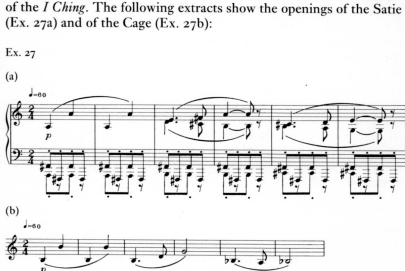

(b)

In 1972 Cage orchestrated his piece and provided it with a quite extra-ordinarily demanding rehearsal schedule which stipulates, among other things, that any player found wanting should be asked to leave. By contrast with the individualist anarchy of *Atlas eclipticalis*, *Cheap Imitation* is a model of a society where all work together towards the achievement of a firm common aim. The promise of McLuhan and Fuller has been replaced by the practice of Mao, for whose policies Cage begins from this period to voice his support.

Also important to the change in his thinking around 1970 were the writings of Thoreau, who provided texts for the *Song Books* (1970), a collection of ninety solos which is in variety of notation a vocal counterpart to the *Concert for Piano and Orchestra*, and also for *Mureau* (1970), which, like the *Sixty-Two Mesostics re Merce Cunningham* (1971), was intended principally for Cage himself to perform as vocalist, a role at which he had arrived through a number of lectures from the 1950s that are more performance than instruction. He also turned to Thoreau for line drawings of natural phenomena to be traced as graphic notation in *Score (Forty Drawings by Thoreau) and Twenty-three Parts* (1974) and in *Renga* (1976).

Thoreau's relevance to Cage, acknowledged not just in these works but in a great many others from the period of renewed productivity that followed *Cheap Imitation*, is both practical and political. The writer's close observation of nature and his resourcefulness in building a harmonious relationship with natural forces held an obvious appeal for a composer still intent on 'imitating nature in her manner of opera-tion', especially at a time when it was becoming clear that techno-logical progress must be limited by the stocks and needs of the earth. On the other front, Thoreau's view that 'the best government is no government' fell in accord with Cage's own long-held opinion, no doubt reinforced by happenings during the Nixon presidency. Moreover, both Thoreau and Mao provided the lesson that attention to specific tasks might be more profitable than proposing grand plans for world improvement, and the few all-embracing protean projects of the 1960s were succeeded in the next decade by a large output of works of more defined aim.

Several of these take up the theme of attunement between nature and technology in a kind of whole-foods music for organic materials. *Child of Tree* (1975) and its development *Branches* (1976) are verbal scores conceived solely for vegetable instruments, such as pod rattles, wood percussion or (and these are obligatory) cactuses amplified so that one can hear the sounds of their spines vibrating. The concern for 'small sounds' here is in the same generous spirit of *Williams Mix* and *Cartridge Music*; the new feature is the use of electronics in a cherishing of nature, with the composer withdrawing from the scene in a touching awareness of his own limited function as intermediary between the performer and his living or once-living instrumentarium, for by contrast with such earlier scores as *4′ 33″ No. 2* or *Variations V*, where the remarks, even though unassuming, have the force of capital letters and clear script, *Child of Tree* and *Branches* are printed as scrawled drafts, bearing all the evidence of changes of mind and second thoughts. The same is true of *Inlets* (1977) for four conch players and the sound of pine cones burning, which last may be presented on tape, as is necessary with the sounds of bird songs in *Telephones and Birds* (1977), of meteorological conditions in *Lecture on the Weather* (1975), and of dawn at the composer's home in *Score . . . and Twenty-three Parts*, to mention just a few of Cage's other ecological treatises.

Score . . . and Twenty-three Parts also belongs with a group of works in which, as in other pieces from as far back as the *Concert for Piano and Orchestra*, Cage has used the orchestra as a model of society; and it says much for his continuing preoccupation with social comportment that he should have returned to this matter so often in the 1970s: in *Cheap Imitation*, in *Etcetera*, in *Score . . . and Twenty-three Parts*, in the set of *Quartets*, and in *Renga*. All four of the later works here replace the strict determinations and controls of *Cheap Imitation* with open opportunities looking back more to *Atlas eclipticalis*, for the Thoreau drawings presented as notation in *Renga* are hardly more limiting than the star-map designs of the earlier work. However, the suggestion that the instrumental sounds should change while they are being produced implies a thoughtful engagement on the part of the player such as Cage had hoped to avoid in *Atlas eclipticalis*, and the work's title, borrowed from a Japanese form of collaborative poetry which calls for contributors to sink their individualities in order to allow the greatest possible scope for others, would indicate a corporate sense no less disciplined than that of *Cheap Imitation*. Anarchy in these more difficult times, one may infer, must be more circumspect and acknowledge the need for common assent.

Renga was composed in answer to a commission from the New York Philharmonic for a work to celebrate the bicentenary of American independence, and at the first performances it was combined with *Apartment House 1776*, which provides for the performance of Revolution-period American music with *I Ching*-determined subtractions, together with vocal interventions from representatives of native and immigrant cultures, Protestant, Sephardic, American Indian, and Black. When *Renga* is played to mark other occasions Cage suggests the use of other appropriate discrepant material with it, either monophonic parallels in the manner of *Cheap Imitation* and of the subsequent 'cheap imitations' contained in the *Song Books* (among which is one contribution from a reworked Queen of the Night) or else defective versions in the style of *Apartment House 1776*. But there is a crucial difference between the first *Cheap Imitation* and the later run-down realizations. Where Cage's Socratic monologue can be understood without irony as a homage to Satie, taking the music into a realm of calm poverty that its composer might have recognized as his own, the presentation of the eighteenth-century pieces of *Apartment House 1776* with elements missing is bound to seem more of a criticism. Though Cage's title would suggest that these are the half-remembered versions of pieces heard from a mansion block of musicians after a gap of two centuries, the original music is in effect deprived of its confidence, and the implicit message is that the American Revolution remains unfinished business.

As long ago as 1949 Cage had declared: 'A finished work is exactly that, requires resurrection.' But only lately has he tried to rectify matters, not only in *Apartment House 1776* but also in *Some of 'The Harmony of Maine' (William Billings) Rewritten* (1978), in the *Hymns and Variations* (also 1978) which practise subtraction on two works, again by Billings, to leave tenuous drifts of choral tone, and again, this time intervening within a literary work, in *Roaratorio, an Irish Circus on Finnegan's Wake* (1979), a second visit after thirty-seven years to the source of *The Wonderful Widow*. Yet the repercussions of subtraction and reworking run well beyond these few works to jolt the whole pattern of Cage's output by throwing a new light on its most consistent feature. Silence had been, from the 1930s, the partner of sound in his rhythmic structures. It then gained a new function, in practice and in retrospect, as the door through which might enter the sounds of the environment. Now its meaning is changed again and it becomes also a signal of omission, suggesting that the written score or the heard music is only a remnant. Comprehended from this new position, the diversity of Cage's production in the 1970s gives no cause for surprise, even when it extends from sets of 'waltzes' which are simply triplets of printed addresses (*Forty-nine Waltzes for the Five Boroughs*, 1977; *A Dip in the Lake*, 1978) to almost conventionally notated works like the *Etudes australes* for piano (1974–5), where the sounds are derived from star maps as in *Atlas eclipticalis* but now transcribed in the fuller manner of *Music for Piano* and *Winter Music*. For where works of the former kind are quite obviously unfinished, those of the latter variety must join Cage's other compositions in seeming like the ruins or embryonic shapes of things which, had circumstances been more propitious, might have been more imposing. And that classic Cage invention *4′ 33″*, now viewed as the subtraction to zero, is not just a window into the world of non-intended sound but also potentially, as Ives once foresaw in prophesying a utopian anarchy in which artists are no longer needed, it is for each individual his own symphony.

LIST OF WORKS

Except where stated scores are published by the Henmar Press of New York.

Three Songs (Stein) for voice and piano, 1932, unpublished: 'Twenty years after', 'It is as it was', 'At east and ingredients'

Sonata for clarinet, 1933

Sonata for Two Voices (of ranges c'–c''' and c–c'') for any two or more instruments, 1933

Solo with Obbligato Accompaniment of Two Voices in Canon, and Six Short Inventions on the Subjects of the Solo (all within range g'–g'') for any three or more instruments, 1933–4; Six Short Inventions scored for trios drawn from ensemble of alto flute, clarinet, trumpet, violin, two violas, and cello, 1958

Composition for Three Voices (of ranges d'–d''', a–a'', and d–d'') for any three or more instruments, 1934

Music for Xenia for piano, 1934, unpublished

Quartet for any percussion, 1935

Quest for piano, 1935, only second movement published

Three Pieces for two flutes, 1935

Two Pieces for piano, *c.*1935, revised 1974

Trio for percussion, 1936; third movement included in *Amores*, 1943

Metamorphosis for piano, 1938

Five Songs (Cummings) for contralto and piano, 1938

Music for Wind Instruments, for flute, clarinet, and bassoon (I), oboe and horn (II), and full quintet (III), 1938

Imaginary Landscape No. 1 for percussion quartet with gramophones, 1939

First Construction (in Metal) for percussion sextet, 1939

Second Construction for percussion quartet, 1940

Bacchanale for prepared piano, 1940

Living Room Music (Stein) for four percussionist-speakers, one also playing melody instrument, 1940

Third Construction for percussion quartet, 1941

Double Music for percussion quartet, in collaboration with Lou Harrison, 1941

Imaginary Landscape No. 2 or *March No. 1* for percussion quintet with electric devices, 1942

Imaginary Landscape No. 3 for percussion sextet with electric devices, 1942

Credo in Us for percussion quartet with electric devices, 1942

And the Earth Shall Bear Again for prepared piano, 1942

Forever and Sunsmell (Cummings) for voice and percussion duo, 1942

In the Name of the Holocaust for prepared piano, 1942

Primitive for string piano, 1942

The Wonderful Widow of Eighteen Springs (Joyce) for voice and closed piano, 1942

Amores for prepared piano (movements I and IV) and percussion trio (movements II and III), movement III 1936 (from Trio), remainder 1943

Our Spring Will Come for piano, 1943

She is Asleep, concert, 1943: 1. Quartet for twelve tom-toms, 2. Duet (textless) for voice and prepared piano, 3. *A Room* for piano or prepared piano

Tossed as it is Untroubled for prepared piano, 1943

Totem Ancestor for prepared piano, 1943

The Perilous Night for prepared piano, 1943–4

A Book of Music for two prepared pianos, 1944
Prelude for Meditation for prepared piano, 1944
Root of an Unfocus for prepared piano, 1944
Spontaneous Earth for prepared piano, 1944
The Unavailable Memory of for prepared piano, 1944
A Valentine out of Season for prepared piano, 1944
Three Dances for two prepared pianos, 1944-5
Daughters of the Lonesome Isle for prepared piano, 1945
Experiences No. 1 for two pianos, 1945
Mysterious Adventure for prepared piano, 1945
Ophelia for piano, 1946
Two Pieces for piano, 1946
Music for Marcel Duchamp for prepared piano, 1947
Nocturne for violin and piano, 1947
The Seasons for orchestra or piano, 1947, only piano version published
Sonatas and Interludes for prepared piano, 1946-8
Dream for piano, 1948
Experiences No. 2 (Cummings) for voice, 1948
In a Landscape for harp or piano, 1948
Suite for Toy Piano (or piano), 1948
String Quartet in Four Parts, 1949-50
Six Melodies for violin and piano, 1950
A Flower (textless) for voice and closed piano, 1950
Concerto for prepared piano and chamber orchestra, 1950-1
Sixteen Dances for flute, trumpet, piano, violin, cello, and percussion quartet, 1951, unpublished
Imaginary Landscape No. 4 or *March No. 2* for twelve radios (twenty-four players), 1951
Music of Changes for piano, 1951
Two Pastorales for prepared piano, 1951-2
Waiting for piano, 1952
Imaginary Landscape No. 5 for any forty-two recordings, 1952
Seven Haiku for piano, 1952
Water Music for pianist, 1952
Williams Mix for tape, 1952, unpublished
For M.C. and D.T. for piano, 1952
4′ 33″ for any instrument or ensemble, 1952
Music for Carillon No. 1, 1952
Music for Piano 1, 1952
Music for Piano 2, 1953
Music for Piano 3, 1953
Music for Piano 4-19 for solo or ensemble, 1953
59½″ for a string player, 1953
Music for Piano 20, 1953
Music for Carillon Nos. 2-3, 1954
31′ 57.9864″ for pianist, 1954
34′ 46.776″ for pianist, 1954
26′ 1.1499″ for a string player, 1953 and 1955
Speech for five radios and newsreader, 1955
Music for Piano 21-36 for solo or ensemble, 1955

Music for Piano 37–52 for solo or ensemble, 1955
27′ 10.554″ for percussionist, 1956
Music for Piano 53–68 for solo or ensemble, 1956
Music for Piano 69–84 for solo or ensemble, 1956
Radio Music for up to eight radios, 1956
Winter Music for up to twenty pianos, 1957
For Paul Taylor and Anita Dencks for piano, 1957
Concert for Piano and Orchestra consisting of solos for piano and thirteen other
 instruments to be played in any combination, 1957–8
Variations I for any number of players, any sound-producing means, 1958
Solo for Voice 1, 1958
Music Walk for one or more pianists, 1958
TV Köln for piano, 1958
Fontana Mix for any means, 1958, tape version 1958–9
Aria for voice, 1958
Sounds of Venice for solo television performance, 1959, unpublished
Water Walk for solo television performance, 1959
Theatre Piece for up to eight performers, 1960
WBAI, auxiliary score for use with other pieces, 1960
Music for 'The Marrying Maiden' (play by Jackson MacLow) for tape, 1960
Solo for Voice 2, 1960
Cartridge Music for amplified sounds (any number of players), 1960
Music for Amplified Toy Pianos, 1960
Music for Carillon No. 4, 1961
Variations II for any number of players, any sound-producing means, 1961
Atlas eclipticalis for up to eighty-six instruments, 1961–2
4′ 33″ No. 2 or *0′ 0″*, solo to be performed in any way by anyone, 1962
Variations III for one or any number of people performing any actions, 1962–3
Variations IV for any number of players, any sounds or combinations of sounds
 produced by any means, with or without other activities, 1963
Electronic Music for Piano for piano with electronics, 1964
Rozart Mix for tape loops, 1965
Variations V, thirty-seven remarks re an audio-visual performance, 1965
Variations VI for a plurality of sound-systems (any sources, components, and loud-
 speakers), 1966
Variations VII for various means, 1966, unpublished
Music for Carillon No. 5, 1967
Musicircus for diverse performers, 1967, unpublished
Newport Mix for tape loops, 1967, unpublished
Reunion for diverse performers, 1968, unpublished
HPSCHD for up to seven harpsichords, up to fifty-one tapes, and other phenomena
 ad lib, composed in collaboration with Lejaren Hiller, 1967–9, unpublished
Sound Anonymously Received for an unsolicited instrument, 1969, unpublished
33 ⅓ for records and gramophones, 1969
Cheap Imitation for piano, 1969; arranged for orchestra of twenty-four, fifty-nine, or
 ninety-five players, 1972, unpublished, and for violin, 1977
Song Books or *Solos for Voice 3–92*, 1970
Mureau for voice, 1970
Les Chants de Maldoror pulverisés par l'assistance même for francophone audience,
 1971, unpublished

Sixty-two Mesostics re Merce Cunningham for voice, 1971

WGBH-TV for composer and technicians, 1971

Bird Cage for tapes with solo performer, 1972

Etcetera for orchestra of any size and tape, 1973, unpublished

Score (Forty Drawings by Thoreau) and Twenty-three Parts for any instruments and/or voices, 1974, unpublished

Etudes australes for piano, 1974-5

Child of Tree (Improvisation I) for percussionist using amplified plant materials, 1975

Lecture on the Weather for twelve performers with independent sound-systems, recordings, and film, 1975, unpublished

Apartment House 1776 for any number of musicians, 1976, unpublished

Branches for percussion solo or ensemble using amplified plant materials, 1976

Quartets I-VIII for twenty-four, forty-one, or ninety-three instruments, 1976, unpublished; versions for concert band and twelve amplified voices, 1976 (I), 1977 (V, VI), all unpublished

Renga for up to seventy-eight instruments and/or voices, 1976, unpublished

Inlets (Improvisation II) for four conch players and the sound of fire, 1977

Telephones and Birds for three performers with telephone announcements and recordings, 1977

Forty-nine Waltzes for the Five Boroughs for performer(s) or listener(s) or record maker(s), 1977

Chorals for violin, 1978, unpublished

A Dip in the Lake: Ten Quicksteps, Sixty-Two Waltzes, and Fifty-Six Marches for Chicago and Vicinity for performer(s) or listener(s) or record maker(s), 1978

Variations VIII for no music or recordings, 1978

Pools for conch shells and tape, 1978, unpublished

Some of 'The Harmony of Maine' (William Billings) Rewritten for organ with three assistants, 1978, unpublished

Letters to Erik Satie for voice and tape, 1978, unpublished

Il treno, three happenings for prepared trains, 1978, unpublished

Someday, ten-hour radio event, 1978, unpublished

Hymns and Variations for twelve amplified voices, 1978

Freeman Etudes for violin, 1978 (I-XVI), 1979- (XVII-XXXII), all unpublished

Etudes boréales for cello and/or piano, 1978-9, unpublished

------, -------- *Circus on* ----------, means for translating a book into music, 1979, unpublished; realization: *Roaratorio, an Irish Circus on Finnegans Wake*, in collaboration with John Fulleman, 1979

Improvisation III, 1980

Improvisation IV, 1980

Litany for the Whale for two voices, 1980

Thirty Pieces for Five Orchestras, 1981

BIBLIOGRAPHY

Writings by Cage

Short notes on his own works are contained in the catalogue issued by the Henmar Press, *John Cage* (New York, 1962). Otherwise the majority of Cage's writings are to be found in four anthologies:

Silence (Middletown, Conn., 1961; London, 1968)
A Year from Monday (Middletown, Conn., 1967; London, 1968)
M (Middletown, Conn., 1973; London, 1973)
Empty Words (London and Boston, 1980)
A further selection is included in *John Cage*, ed. Richard Kostelanetz (New York, 1970; London, 1971).

Cage was also the co-author with Kathleen Hoover of *Virgil Thomson* (New York, 1959) and the co-editor with Alison Knowles of a volume reproducing manuscripts by diverse contemporary composers, *Notations* (New York, 1969).

Writings on Cage

Cage's work has stimulated an enormous literature of essays and reviews. Many of the more valuable items are included in Kostelanetz (see above), in *Musik-Konzepte: Sonderband John Cage* (Munich, 1978), and in Daniel Charles's *Gloses sur John Cage* (Paris, 1978). Charles has also published a volume of interviews with Cage as *Pour les Oiseaux* (Paris, 1976).